First World War
and Army of Occupation
War Diary
France, Belgium and Germany

9 DIVISION
1 Lowland Brigades
Brigade Trench Mortar Battery
20 April 1919 - 31 August 1919

WO95/1776/5

The Naval & Military Press Ltd
www.nmarchive.com
Published in association with The National Archives

Published by

The Naval & Military Press Ltd

Unit 10 Ridgewood Industrial Park,

Uckfield, East Sussex,

TN22 5QE England

Tel: +44 (0) 1825 749494

www.naval-military-press.com

www.nmarchive.com

This diary has been reprinted in facsimile from the original. Any imperfections are inevitably reproduced and the quality may fall short of modern type and cartographic standards.

© **Crown Copyright**
Images reproduced by permission of The National Archives, London, England, 2015.

Contents

Document type	Place/Title	Date From	Date To
Heading	Lowland (Late 9) Division 1st Lowland Bde Trench Mortar Batty 1919 Apr-1919 Aug		
War Diary	Solingen	20/04/1919	18/06/1919
War Diary	Central	19/06/1919	03/07/1919
War Diary	Solingen	04/07/1919	10/07/1919
War Diary	Hackenbraick	11/07/1919	29/07/1919
Heading	War Diary of 1st Lowland Bde Trench Mortar Battery 1st To 31st August 1919		
War Diary	Hackenbraick	30/07/1919	31/08/1919

LOWLAND (LATE 9) DIVISION

1st LOWLAND BDE

TRENCH MORTAR BATTY

1919 APR — 1919 AUG

WAR DIARY
or
INTELLIGENCE SUMMARY.
(Erase heading not required.)

Army Form C. 2118.

Place	Date	Hour	Summary of Events and Information	Remarks and references to Appendices
Solingen	20/7/19	0845-12.30	Battery Training carried out after Training Programme	
do	20/7/19	do	do do do ant. orders dated 2/7/19 1/5/22	
			dated 2/7/19 received + acknowledged) in Defence Scheme No 22. (Intentions made	
			accordingly)	
Solingen	1/5/19	0845-12.30	Battery Training carried out after Training Programme	
do	2/5/19	do	do	
do	3/5/19	do	do (Clover Corps ft.	
			Defence Scheme No 22 received and acknowledged (Ott. 6744 destroyed at	
			ten instructions (P. m. 1. 8/22 dated 3/5/19	
Solingen	4/5/19	0945-11.00	Rifles Inspection and Church Parade.	
do	5/5/19	0845-12.30	Battery Training carried out after Training Programme	
do	6/5/19	do	do	
do	7/5/19	do	do	
do	8/5/19	do	do	
do	9/5/19	do	do	
do	10/5/19	do	Sun Evening Interior Economy (Carried out in Billets (Relate Sv.)	

WAR DIARY
or
INTELLIGENCE SUMMARY

Army Form C. 2118.

(Erase heading not required.)

Place	Date	Hour	Summary of Events and Information	Remarks and references to Appendices
Solingen	11/5/19	09.45	Rifles Inspection and Church Parade	
do	12/5/19	08.45 12.30	Fatigue Training carried out after Programme, also 16.0) Lecture by Sgt Instructor Gill. "The history of our Parliament"	
do	13/5/19	08.45 12.30	do	
do	14/5/19	do	do	see notes by 2/Lt Thomson on Versailles Term
do	15/5/19	do	on Oben Marsan	
Solingen	15/5/19	do	Fatigue Training carried out as per Training Programme	
do	16/5/19	do	do	
do	17/5/19	do	Gun Cleaning, Interior Economy (Rifles, Schulz, Lx)	
do	18/5/19	09.45 11.00	Rifles Inspection Church Parade	
do	19/5/19	05.45 12.30	Fatigue Training as per Training Programme	
do	20/5/19	do	do	see Lecture by Col Commdg
do			Lt's Educational LEO (One Lecture to our Coombry)	
Solingen	21/5/19	do	Fatigue Training carried out as per Training Programme	do
do	22/5/19	do	do	do
do	23/5/19	do	On Inspection of Ammunition	do

WAR DIARY or INTELLIGENCE SUMMARY

Army Form C. 2118.

Place	Date	Hour	Summary of Events and Information	Remarks and references to Appendices
Solingen	24/5/19	0845	Curt Olming. Interior Economy.	
"	25/5/19	"	Divine Service. Church Parade (Rifle Schule Sta.)	
			(Ref. map Germany 2.B. 1,100,000 Elberfeld 1/25000). Direction for Advance into Germany	
			reconnaissance made for complying with same.	
			75 Tracks booked to U.K. on leave.	
Solingen	26/5/19	"	Easter Training carried out as per Programme.	
"	27/5/19	"	Route march (sandwich trees) also drilled for Advance into	
			Germany (Ref. map Solingen sheet 1/25000 received and acknowledged	
"	28/5/19	"	Tactical Scheme.	
"	29/5/19	"	Battery Training. Western hof Thomen Datum point)	

Lewis Llewellyn Lt.
a/OC F (Howard) T.M.B.

Army Form C. 2118.

WAR DIARY
or
INTELLIGENCE SUMMARY.
(Erase heading not required.)

Instructions regarding War Diaries and Intelligence Summaries are contained in F. S. Regs., Part II. and the Staff Manual respectively. Title pages will be prepared in manuscript.

Place	Date	Hour	Summary of Events and Information	Remarks and references to Appendices
Jalunger	30/9	0800	Battery carrying out drill Programme.	
do	31/9	1215	do	
do	1/9	1000	Divine Service and Lecture.	
do		1100	Church Parade	
do	2/9	0800	do	
do		1215	Battery carrying out Training Programme	
do	3/9	do	Route March.	
do	4/9	do	Lecture. Steam.	
do	5/9	do	Battery carrying out ordinary Programme and Lecture Rifle Service	
do	6/9	do	do	
do	7/9	do	River Blanira and Interior Economy	
do	8/9	1000	do	
do		1100	Church Parade.	
do	9/9	0800	Battery carrying out ordinary Programme, Lecture Rifle Thomson	
do		1215		
do	10/9	do	do	and use of both Command	
do	11/9	do	Lecture. Steam.	
do	12/9	do	Battery carrying out ordinary Programme	
do		do	do	
			Leave to U.K.	

A6945 Wt. W11422/M1160 350,000 12/16 D.D.&I. Forms/C./2118/14.

WAR DIARY
or
INTELLIGENCE SUMMARY.
(Erase heading not required.)

Army Form C. 2118.

Place	Date	Hour	Summary of Events and Information	Remarks and references to Appendices

WAR DIARY
INTELLIGENCE SUMMARY
(Erase heading not required.)

Army Form C. 2118.

Place	Date	Hour	Summary of Events and Information	Remarks and references to Appendices
Broots	26/9	0800	Brothox Tramining Carried out for Infantry (1 Platoon & one other Rank)	
do	27/9	do	Brothox Training Carried out as per Programme	
do	28/9	do	Gun Cleaning & Interior Economy	
do	do	08.15	Rcvd 18/719 reverse at Divisional repts	

George Morrison
Coming Lieutenant for O.M.G.

Army Form C. 2118.

WAR DIARY
or
INTELLIGENCE SUMMARY.
(Erase heading not required.)

Instructions regarding War Diaries and Intelligence Summaries are contained in F.S. Regs., Part II. and the Staff Manual respectively. Title pages will be prepared in manuscript.

Place	Date	Hour	Summary of Events and Information	Remarks and references to Appendices
Bailieul	30/10	08.45	Ration Training carried out as per Programme.	
do	1/10	12.45	Do.	
do	2/10	Do.	Do.	
do	3/10	14.00 / 16.00	March from Brobaix to Lingen	
Lingen	4/10	08.45 / 14.45	Battery Training carried out as per Programme	
do	5/10	Do.	Do.	
do	6/10	10.00 / 11.00	Church Parade	
do	7/10	12.45	Battery training carried out as per Programme	
do	8/10	Do.	Do.	
do	9/10	Do.	Do.	
do	10/10	06.00 / 17.00	March from Lingen to Karlstrul	
Karlstrul	11/10	08.45 / 12.45	Battery training carried out as per programme	
do	12/10	Do.	Do.	
do	13/10	10.00 / 11.00	Church Parade	
do	14/10	08.45 / 12.45	Battery training carried out as per programme	
do	15/10	Do.	Do.	

WAR DIARY
or
INTELLIGENCE SUMMARY.

(Erase heading not required.)

Army Form C. 2118.

Place	Date	Hour	Summary of Events and Information	Remarks and references to Appendices
Steenbecque	16/2/19	05.45 12.45	Battery Training carried out as per Programme.	M24
Do.	17/2/19	Do.	Do.	
Do.	18/2/19	Do.	Do.	
Do.	19/2/19	Do.	Do.	
Do.	20/2/19	10.00 11.00	Church Parade	M25
Do.	21/2/19	08.45 12.45	Battery Training carried out as per Programme.	M26
Do.	22/2/19	Do.	Do.	
Do.	23/2/19	Do.	Do.	
Do.	24/2/19	Do.	Do.	
Do.	25/2/19	Do.	Do.	
Do.	26/2/19	Do.	Do.	
Do.	27/2/19	10.00 11.00	Church Parade	M27
Do.	28/2/19	08.45 12.45	Battery Training carried out as per Programme.	M28
Do.	30/2/19	Do.	Do.	

War Diary
of
1st Lowland Trench Mortar Battery
1st to 31st August 1919

Army Form C. 2118.

WAR DIARY
or
INTELLIGENCE SUMMARY.
(Erase heading not required.)

Instructions regarding War Diaries and Intelligence Summaries are contained in F.S. Regs., Part II. and the Staff Manual respectively. Title pages will be prepared in manuscript.

Place	Date	Hour	Summary of Events and Information	Remarks and references to Appendices
Rollestone	30/9	09.45	Battery turned over after Training Programme	
do	31/9	12.45	do	
do	1/10	do	do	
do	2/10	do	Gun Drill and Interior Economy	
do	3/10	10.00	Short Parade	
do	4/10	11.03	Route Estimate	
do	5/10	09.45	Battery turned out after Training Programme	
do	6/10	12.45	do	
do	7/10	do	do	
do	8/10	do	do	
do	9/10	do	do	
do	10/10	10.00	Church Parade	
do	11/10	11.00	Battery Turning carried out after Training Programme	
do	12/10	12.45	do	
do	13/10	do	do	
do	14/10	do	Preparations for Route March etc to T.M. Practice Camp	

Army Form C. 2118.

WAR DIARY
or
INTELLIGENCE SUMMARY.
(Erase heading not required.)

Instructions regarding War Diaries and Intelligence Summaries are contained in F. S. Regs., Part II and the Staff Manual respectively. Title pages will be prepared in manuscript.

Place	Date	Hour	Summary of Events and Information	Remarks and references to Appendices
Lockinge	15.19	12.45	Battalion Training for 1st Scotland Rifle Sports	
Do	16		Do	
Do	17	10.00	Church Parade	
Do		11.00	Do	
Do	18	10.45 12.45	Training & Training for Scotland Rifle Sports	
Do	19		Do	
Do	20		Do	
Do	21		Do	
Do	22		Do	
Do	23		Church Parade	
Do	24	10.00 11.00	Do	
Do	25	08.45 12.45	Pioneers for Sports (1 Scotland Rifle Sports)	
Do	26	Do	Training carried out after Evening programme	
Do	27	Do	Do	
Do	28	Do	Do	
Do	29	Do	Do	
Do	30			

Army Form C. 2118.

WAR DIARY
or
INTELLIGENCE SUMMARY.
(Erase heading not required.)

Instructions regarding War Diaries and Intelligence Summaries are contained in F. S. Regs., Part II. and the Staff Manual respectively. Title pages will be prepared in manuscript.

Place	Date	Hour	Summary of Events and Information	Remarks and references to Appendices

www.ingramcontent.com/pod-product-compliance
Lightning Source LLC
Chambersburg PA
CBHW081518160426

43193CB00014B/2726